Therapy in the Wind

An Illustrated Anthology of Nature Poems

by Clients and Therapists

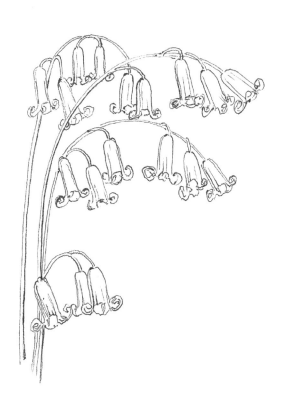

Curated and edited by Claire de la Varre

POSITIVE SPIRAL PRESS, CHAPEL HILL

For everyone who has ever stepped outside, breathed fresh air, looked at the clouds or the stars, talked to trees or animals, walked barefoot on the earth, or felt the healing power of sunlight, moonlight, rain, or the sea.

In between birth and death,
there is such a short time for singing.
~ Helen Percy

Foreword

In 2019, I attended a residential programme in Shining Cliff Woods, Derbyshire, called Taking Therapy Outside. Our group of twelve therapists stayed in a cabin, and cooked and ate communally. We gathered around a firepit, spent a rainy day in a beech wood, journalled, wrote and recited our poetry, and did therapy in pairs. Daily, we walked into the woods on our own to explore our responses to nature using the surroundings as metaphor. The seed for this book was planted then.

Recognition is spreading that exposure to the natural world is therapeutic. A growing body of research provides evidence for the benefits of spending time in green spaces, going outside, and even from bringing plants into our houses and schools.

It can be liberating, inspiring, and even transformational to walk outside, breathe deeply, and swing arms and legs in steady rhythm. We can look down and pay attention to the small things like leaves, grass, flowers, mud, and insects. When we turn our attention upwards and outwards, we connect to the larger world—trees, lakes, mountains, clouds, the ocean, the weather, the sun, the moon, and the stars and reflect on our place in it.

We may venture into nature alone, relishing the silence, or with friends or loved ones, as we move into deeper conversation. Perhaps we take along a dog or two, companions that offer another way of being, completely embodied and present in the moment. The greens, browns and blues of nature soothe and restore us, often bringing new perspective and clarity of mind.

But although nature may heal us, who is healing nature? Humans are destroying the earth through greed and ignorance in a multitude of careless and heartbreaking ways.

That damage is perpetuated across multiple generations. We may feel disconnected, lonely, depressed, abandoned, hopeless, despairing, or suicidal. We attempt to escape through addictive, repetitive, or compulsive behaviours that ultimately make us feel worse. The struggle with mental health is familiar to many, and some of us seek the help of a therapist – a professional who can listen and facilitate change and healing, detraumatise the past, and increase self-awareness.

This anthology encompasses a broad range of human experiences and emotions, from joy to deep grief. It has been created by people who are therapists, as well as those who have benefitted from therapy. Some of us fall into both categories. All contributors—writers, poets, and artists—have experienced firsthand the power of nature to heal, inspire and uplift. Just as you can enjoy singing without being a professional, you do not need to have a degree in creative writing to enjoy the benefits of poetry. The act of writing poetry is often therapeutic, and writing poems about nature allows us to re-experience or extract deeper meaning from our encounters.

This book is written for you—enjoy it!

And go outside...

~ Claire de la Varre

Table of Contents

The Poems

Poems by Diana Thornton

One of my earliest memories of school is of standing at the edge of the school field at the age of six or seven, gazing at the horizon where the Derbyshire moorland met the sky and gaining solace from it. Perhaps I was a strange, solitary child but I still feel a primitive, visceral homecoming whenever I am back in the Peak District. That ability of the natural world to soothe, comfort and inspire me is not limited to the north of England but is readily available wherever I am if I just pause for long enough to mesh with those natural rhythms around me and lose myself once again in nature's realm.

I am a mindfulness teacher and a Human Givens Therapist. The mindfulness puts structure and language around something which I intuited as a child: that paying attention to nature puts us in touch with a deep stillness; a source of delight, of surprise and even joy. I have found at times that it can open us to that sense of belonging, of taking our place in this organic profusion around us and of our deep connectedness to it. I often work with people who are feeling closed down, numb or in pain. I encourage my clients to take the time to savour and relish the natural world; not only those big moments of a fabulous sunset or a stunning vista but the tiny things which may pass us by unless we make a conscious decision to stop and pay attention to them. There is a danger of sounding like Julie Andrews singing about raindrops on roses but there is nothing saccharine about the pure drops of nourishment which are available to us if we just take the time to notice. When we are feeling parched, single drops are what we need to soften the dry, hard earth.

Autumn Dog Walk

A tweedy butterfly from this year's autumn collection
lands on the path to bask in the sun.
An arresting haute couture outline thrown incongruous into this
day of jumpers and jeans.

A heavy bumblebee, having taken her autumnal pledge and
intoxicated by this final binge,
buzzes too loud and cannot steer;
collides with my forehead and loops away genially.
Birdsong eases from the trees.
No longer a strident call for mates
but relief that last night's first frost
has been vanquished by this stolen day of sun.

Walking uphill a chimera of spring as bright green beech leaves flirt
with the sun
like coquettish young girls.
But that's from beneath.
From above they reveal their dark green leathery skins, their veins
and the creep of dryness,
their menopausal phase revealed.

Ridiculous props were installed overnight to dress the woods for this
harvest parade.
Dewy webs draped between stalks of grass thick and spun like heavy
candyfloss.
Pristine toadstools, with spotty reds and tiny oranges, lend Enid
Blyton charm.

The dogs and their people smile.
We know what's coming. But not today.

Epigenetics

How does this dragonfly know how to fly?

So recently the terror of tadpoles but on this bright blue day
transformed with mysterious knowledge; scything and diving to
terrorise flies with ferocious ease and grace.

And I stand transfixed.

Transformed with mysterious knowledge of what beauty is, the
ancestral lineage of delight and joy which well up with the ease of an
instinct and the grace of a gift.

Wisp

This wisp of stardust I call me is like an eddy in the stream; held by some mysterious centrifugal force. But one day these borrowed atoms will burst free to find another constellation and life will flow in different form.

This hand of mine which writes now with this pen perhaps has atoms from a long dead whale or unfurled as a new shoot in sun. The stuff of me has maybe taken flight and ridden currents vertiginous and free or secret burrowed under soft dark earth.

No wonder to feel at ease when I'm outside. My body resonates with recognition of its kin.

Death then is nothing but a stirring of the stream for life flows on and we should dance and sing when it's our turn because we are the only ones who know we can.

When Daffodils Die

I do not grieve when daffodils die for I am assured that they will come again, just as they did last year.

And looking from this casement window their essential daffodillyness would seem the same as years roll by.

I cling to the idea that my life should have some goal, some product to demonstrate time well spent, but I am just one season's bloom.

The grand maternal floriference long gone, and my children's foliage, hold me in my season's place. My purpose is simply to flower.

No need to mourn. Spring follows and life flows on in endless rearrangement of constancy.

Letter to Myself

There is tenderness in the earth and in the natural order of things. Hush and listen and you will hear the gentle patterns your mind craves. The way of being is the same for a mountain, a stream, a thrush, a twig bedecked with lichen and a human soul. We have built a concrete zoo and wonder at our distress and sense of disconnection.

Hush. All will emerge.
The dog and the chickens will point the way.

My Place

I take my place. I am a speck in the universe. Born in the Bang with all matter. Sibling to planets. No need for me to hold on for it holds me.

Here's my space. Right here on this grass where the ground holds me and the sun warms me and the swallows dance overhead.

I take my place. Without fear I let go for the universe holds me as part of itself.

Rupture

I saw a snake this morning as I walked the dog on Oxshott Heath.
The shock and joy which bubbled from my belly erupted as a laugh.

I heard her first. A leafy portamento which could only mean a
snake – perhaps a slow-worm. And so I looked.

I had been looking up through startling green of leaves
transformed by powerful rays of light with blue beyond.
Somehow my ears and soul were opened too through seeing and
so I heard her and looked down.

She seemed incongruous here in KT22 and it was that which
stripped me back to let the beauty of a brown and inconspicuous
creature rupture my isolation; let me be as one with these
familiar woods.

The leafy staccato of a blackbird revealed a creature just as stunning.

Silence

There are places so still that you can hear an ancient silence. The silence in which these trees have grown cell by cell.

The silent presence of this wall as it has gently gathered feathers of moss.

Sound which marks the hours with rhythm and cadence, passing time.

Silence which listens to all eternity caught in this brief moment, lost and found again.

Like a rivet piling deep through centuries past, it pierces all moments to bind forgotten thens with now.

Clients and Therapists

Poems by Kim Smith Stout

In times of emotional angst, scraps of poems come to mind like bubbles in a hot spring. There they percolate, until retrieved and pulled fully into existence.

Since discovering as a child that nature fosters clarity of mind, I have sought solace and inspiration in the woods. The following poems describe the ending of a long marriage, and the first signs thereafter of a happier life.

river tonic

I am viscera awash in
shallows of deepening gloom
rock me River, rock me.
Anger's building,
on the ruin.
Send me to your deepest drink
brace me with its chill
fill me with the tonic
of your everlasting still.

on having followed
the Pied Piper of Driftingsand

Who would have ever guessed?

Here I am.
In the sun.
Free to chase pelican shadows.

The next time one skims the surf
I might simply rise and lift away.

wide winter

Pray I can cross the wide winter I am wasting from plying the day
the undertow's grip is unflinching and the shoreline a longing away
I would tether my bones to the vulture who proffered a scavenger's fare
oh to glide on a wing into April having dreamlessly slept the way there.

2023   C.G.

*The winter following our separation, I drove past our old house
every day on the way to work. The daffodils that came into bloom
that Spring where I had planted them along the roadside, were a
balm for my heart…*

vestige garden

don't cry

don't cry

look
where your
dull spade cuffed
Carolina clay where
you gathered possibilities
smooth like cream colored
stones in parchment-thin flyaway
wrappings where you paused to marvel
such perfection then tucked them one by
one into the ground where the earth exhaled
with each new promise planted and you savored
every sweet exquisite breath and where twenty
spent Septembers toppled over and with your
family in a downpour washed away
don't cry don't cry
look
cheerful
clumps of
serendipity are
springing through
the blackberry tangle

The daffodils are blooming.

Clients and Therapists

Poems by Betsy Bowen

I live in North Carolina with my husband and Chloe, an African Grey Parrot.

My work has been published in the Pinesong Awards of the North Carolina Poetry Society, the Neuse River Anthology, Between the Lines, Bay Leaves, League of Minnesota Poets, and Pitt Community College Art forum.

Natures amazes, amuses, and humbles me. While I frequently write about beautiful, capricious, and unpredictable nature, I write mostly about the feelings and questions nature evokes.

Pure Gossip?

Mile after mile the trees along the road marshal
trunk-to-trunk, woody dendrites and axons limb
to branch, external neurons of the forest. I wonder

if they play *whisper-down-the-lane*, culminating
in trunk-slapping gibberish somewhere up the road,
or pass only notable tidbits along their aerial highway.

Unseen birds sweeten the air with song, in truth chirping
news and gossip along the highway, perhaps about the Scarlet
Kingsnake midway to exit 104, an appealing appetizer

for the hawk, seemingly aloof and uninterested, weaving
the air on broad thermals, ruddy tail fanned against
a pale-blue curtain. What do the trees learn from the fungi

nestled by their roots? Do they send it twitching neighbor
to neighbor? And time beyond seasons? Have eons
passed since last October when their crimson coronas

fell as embers to the forest floor or does it feel like yesterday
the hawk's ancestral relatives sat hunched on their boughs
while soldiers at Fredericksburg lay dying in their shadows?

Nature, a Universal Language, Understood by All

Two people, a couple perhaps, on the beach
in Costa Rica, perched on a jetty at the edge
of the ocean. Heads bent, bodies stooped
staring down and pointing. My feet bustle
in their direction while others meander
by or sit spellbound by the dancing surf.
An impetuous wave and *Hi!* spills out of me
on my path to their location and I'm reminded
by their response that I am not bilingual,
only curious. And there, stranded
in an almost non-existent tide pool
under the rocks, an octopus smaller
than a clamshell and in danger of parching.
Tiny tentacles akimbo, gray and unmoving,
room key card serving as makeshift stretcher.
I was there for the rescue, part of the drama,
as we safely navigated baby to open water.

The Trades of Hawaii

Trade winds skim the buoyant window
to a kaleidoscope of coral reefs and colorful
fish, then drift across the islands like sweet
whispers in the night, wafting an alchemy
of salt air, ambrosial plumeria and Coppertone,
prompting shadowed promises in hushed tones,
all but forgotten when the breeze tames the sun's
heat and cools the flames of the night's ardor –
passion scatters across the Pacific.

Where are They Now?

Passing by, I watch memories slip
through weary clapboards, spill
onto the porch like kids at play,
and mingle with still vivid dreams
resting there, out front on the overstuffed chair.

Vines forsaking their loamy boundary
tumble across the faded cushions,
no longer puffed with local gossip
or plump with expectation.

Whispers of long-ago life swirl
across the fallow fields. The barn,
there's always a barn or shed nearby,
stands crumpled as an old man leaning
on his cane, shelters only a family
of swallows and a few prayers.

Speed Demon with Attitude

Kona winds skid across the turquoise
Hawaiian surf, creating imposing
liquid meringue peaks. No calming
this beast with hypnotic strokes
to its underbelly.
Palm trees bow, their fronds
blown into balletic poses, and kiss
earthen cheeks. Forty-ton humpback
whales stirred by the excitement,
pirouette – and I swear yell *Yippee!*
as they smack their flukes
on churning waves.

Crows' Good Morning

If they say "good morning"
to each other in terms
couched with cooing
and adoration...
I don't hear it.

Instead I'm awakened
by the ear-splitting blast
of angry crow parents
screaming orders to insolent
crow children.

My eyes closed to the wonder
of dust dancing in the sunbeams,
the brassy discord twitches
through my body, intruding
on my dreams.

Covers overhead, I clutch vestiges
of cocooned slumber, marveling
how nocturnal animals
surrender to the crows
discordant lullaby.

Pondering Oneness

The stream ripples around my feet
the cold water teasing my toes.
Perched on the sun warmed rocks,
old sol and the clouds are busy
playing hide and seek, skittering
across the deep blue of eternity.

Struggling for answers, silliness
takes hold and I am one with a pile
of dirty socks, or a duckbill platypus.
One with the dust balls under my bed
or the dust of my ancestors' bones.

One with stones in the stream,
smooth and soothing in my hand,
and one with stones thrown in hate.
Glimpses of prejudice and rancor
seep into my sun dappled musing
as so much offal. My eyes flood
with rivers of hurt and intolerance.

Overwhelmed, I see myself as a speck
in the cosmos, a miniscule bit of carbon
and wonder who can fix the world.
I give the stone back to the stream
and watch dispassionate circles expand.
Peering into the water for answers
there's only my reflection.

Round Balls and Tall Things

I dream of a bucolic English garden gracing
my half-acre suburban yard. Drifts of color
from cosmos, echinacea, delphiniums lyrical
against the house. Purple clematis climbing
a pergola overlooking the moss verbena creeping
along the flagstone path, standing watch
as spring bulbs burst forth. First narcissus
heralding spring followed by iris in a color
so perfect words fail to relate. Foxglove and
asters in chorus with dahlias along the side
with a deep forest in the back. Pure pastoral
enchantment filled with bird song and whispering
trees. When vision clears I see typical suburban
landscaping with two teams of wannabe round
boxwood taking the front field, a Crepe Myrtle
acting as home plate and arborvitae standing guard
in the outfield. Geometry reigns, yielding no space
for overflowing pots of colorful Begonia, petunias,
impatiens and ivy spilling willy-nilly over the side.

Avoiding Extinction

I. Dinosaur skeletons long hidden
    in earthen Chinese closets.
    Withered bones surrendering
    their story as a crone might recite hers.

    Crowned Dragon they call him. Venerable
    ancestor of Tyrannosaurus Rex. Débuting
    as a world star after one hundred
    and sixty million years of anonymity.

    A fierce eating machine
    stomping into oblivion,
    encumbered with a prodigious
    nasal crest – a seductive pompadour,
    fragile as a teen's heart.

II. Pity the peacock, forever
    dragging a bridal train
    of iridescent feathers.
    All eyes on the sweeping display.

    Or tutti-frutti plumed birds
    with intricate mating dances
    and no Arthur Murray studio
    to instruct the klutz.

    Or forty-pound racks lugged
    everywhere by elk. Velvet gloved
    antlers stripped for battle,
    just for a date …

III.   Lucky us, not saddled
         with cumbersome sexual
         ornamentation. No huge headdress
         to wedge gingerly into a car.

         We taunt the natural
         with self-imposed adornments.
         Color, straighten, cut and curl,
         Hair club and hair plugs.

         Memberships in gyms
         for six-pack abs and trips
         to the spa. All to grease
         the skids of creation.

         What will scientists postulate
         when they unearth the bones
         of our feet distorted from years
         of sexy shoes?

Clients and Therapists

Poems by Elaine Curtin

I grew up surrounded by the beautiful singing voices of my fellow Cork people. With an abundance of family love, I was a child surrounded by chatty adults who knew how and when to use a good, apt story. Tall, passionate grown-ups surrounded me in the vibrant city family shop where my mother worked. Lifelong friends I met at Catholic schools where I learnt about community, faith, atheism, expression, and humour. I was educated in English literature and psychology for my degree. A lyrical world surrounded me, and I learned the power of using well-timed, simple language.

I found my way into the therapy world as a recipient of Human Givens therapy. I was lost in sadness and grief, weighed down by life and confused, until I found my happiness and balance again. Then I started to express myself honestly: the love for and from my daughter; the support of friends and family. Words express my own pictures and my feelings and the thing about words is… they matter.

I met my loving partner in recent years and all of it brought me to where my purpose now is. As a Human Givens therapist, I love the comfortable use of expression, guided imagery and story-telling intrinsic to this pragmatic approach. I tell stories to help others navigate their way through, working with their own metaphorical language which invites me to access their world, images and words.

I write poetry from my heart, the words tumble out, I go back and tweak a little. I write for my friends, my loved ones, my therapy clients. Mostly for myself. It feels a little self-indulgent, but I remind myself I'm simply expressing something important in those moments, then it feels right to share it. I hope you enjoy it too!

Sow a Seed

Sow a seed and watch it grow
Open the earth and dig down low
Scatter the dust and watch it fly
Make a mark, take in our sky.

Take a breath, watch and wait,
The birds, they'll come investigate
Pollinated petals play their tune
And all will float towards our moon.

The bees will buzz, and blossoms shudder
Their brightest hues, flies flap and flutter
Catch the earth, the sea, the shores
The land, the grass, the sun, all yours.

Tall Tree

Rustling, splintering light, and swaying
Bees buzzing, needing cover,
Shade making canopy above my head
Chitter chatter
Over here, to over there, where

Hopping and tweeting all upon us
Me, strong, tall, straight, breath held
No space for soft and to relax here
Upright, tall, bark all over

Claw-like toes, pushing into strong, soft
Red and green earth
A footprint makes solid on the ground
Staircase for smaller crawlers
To climb on, tickling, trickling
No twitching here, no itching here

Holding life, keeping all at bay
All arms held straight, I grow within me
Now, dive on through green sprinkles
Tentacles spreading wide and far
The brown, the mud down below
Stroked, fed, moistened by my woodland friends

Keep me steady, tall, fed, loved,
The lonely, and beloved
Allowing that breath out, flexing
Moving with the chit, the chat
In the air, above, below, here, there
Caressed, stretched, held
Only for them, there would be
Nothing to see.

Yellow

Sprouting up to rising
Tentacles clawing up then down
Grasping their place
Sunshine maker on a bank
Yellowing around surrounds
Slippery bursting buds
Springing sprigs to here
To us
The unknown
Here

Born Again

Feathers sprinkle through the green
And then they leap and fly, so clean
I am bird and travel high above
So think of me when you think 'Love'

I wrap around the bark from roots
Tangling through the branchy shoots
Ivy for the bird to hop up high
So think of me when you think 'Fly'

I am tall and strong and brown
With many arms to spring out from
My tree roots go down deep below
So think of me when you think 'Grow'

I am small and dark and crawl
And nourish dirt that's moist with pall
I'm one of many grubs in the earth
So think of me when you think 'Birth'

Wind

Deep and wide, I move the tide
White tops fly and crash on sand
Carry the birds from side to side
They use my might to move their land.

A whistling howl is my voice
A warning shot when all at sea
Inhale me deep and feel the calm
I'll cool your lungs and make you free.

I leave destruction when it's needed
But clear the air space to make a stop
The power is in how you see me
Take a breath and watch me drop.

My name is Wind, I work with others
The sun, the sea, the earth, all friends
You wail at me, I'll show you fervour
Hold me close, we'll cry, then mend.

Water

Crashing, swelling, falling
Bubbling over lichen creek
Drop to stop at dammed walls
Hear the roar, no cracks to seek

Seeking holes and hidden spaces
Flowing down the stream and follow
Gush to gallop and thunder
To whirl the pools and rock bed hollow

Mellow days waft still with mirrors
Tempest dark swells up and through
Though fish and surfers fly within me
It's clear, there's depth in our blue

Watery to soothe and clean
Carrier of feathers, pebbles and weed
When tapped I quench and oft refresh
On my back to carry charging steed

Waterfall

Stone to back and holds the watcher
Thundering water crashing out front
Steam rising, toes soaked from splashing
Life pushing through, ripping, flowing, forcing

Screaming down, softly scraping face off cliff
Below into lake, calm before gushing out to sea
Bubbling to ocean, upward steam rising, making
Clouds to rain, dampening of dry parched soil

Making rivers out of streams
And then down, down pouring
Thundering, calling, shouting, scoring
Melting to a carpet of water, cleaning

Now, only now, all new
Stand back, be the stone
And watch

Geese

Air punching, water thrashing, wings crashing
Screeching at the sleeping town
Fish or land or life to fight for
Disturbed dreams upside down

Slicing through visions and dropping to water
Is there one, or two or ten?
The wind gets whipped, and stirred and punched
A hullabaloo ensues, and then...

A honking hurricane, goes high and drifts away
Then alone, booming silence fills our space
We wait, stand by, a breath to take
Dropping off, fluttering with grace.

The Pole

A blackbird twirled first left then right
In the blue above up in the bright

A long twig held in beak like pole
Feathers billowing to reach the goal

An erroneous worm or to start a nest
To flutter it so hard beneath her chest

A thing of wonder, a moment to stop
To see it push and pull, then drop

The twig released and fell to ground
And she went higher, lighter

Not a sound.

Poems by Barbara E. Phanjoo

I was born in Lancashire in 1941 and brought up in the Lake District. In 1959 I came to Edinburgh University for an MA in English Language and Literature and a Diploma in Education.

I married a Mauritian medical student in 1963 who later became a consultant psychiatrist. I have three children.

I taught English in Edinburgh secondary schools and for more than 25 years was also a marriage and relationships counsellor, tutor and supervisor. I am still living in Edinburgh and long retired!

Blackbird

In the waning light
A blackbird flings its anthem
On the heedless world,
Telling of joy in the
Heart of sadness
And sadness
In the heart of joy.
Its unselfconscious song
Primordial and ever new,
Like the eternal presence
That looks out at us
In tenderness
From the darkening sky.

2023   C.G.

Sun After Rain

Every leaf is shining.
The rain-spattered windows
Become the Milky Way,
Puddles ripple and turn
Into a thousand abstract
Works of art.
The darkest crevices are pierced.
Fences and wires wear necklaces
And the trees drip drip
Like the Earth's heartbeat.
It is no coincidence
That beaming means smiling!

Chestnut Tree

There was a time
When this was just a tree,
A green shadow that in Summer
Became the lushness
Through my kitchen window.

Now it is much more.
It accompanies me
From day to day
Through the seasons of my year,
A living presence.

It has become a holy thing,
Symbolic in its beauty
Of that predictable, never-failing love
That unfolds through history
For those who would see.

My first prayer at the beginning of each day
Is prompted by its presence
Amid the iron gloom that shades
My winter heart.
Its leaf-lorn branches beckon
And the dove alights,
The source of all creation.

Great sticky buds
Pulsating with eternity
Burst into crinkled greenness.
The candles glow, shining and holy,
Love pierces my heart
In spite of my resistance.

Wind

You, wind,
Slamming against my window,
Grumbling in the chimney
Keeping me awake.

You, wind,
Abusing the last of my roses,
Blowing their petals wide.

You, wind,
Frightening the leaves on the lawn,
Clustering under the hedge.

You, wind,
Parting the billows of the sky,
Letting the moon sail through.

You, wind,
Blowing a gap in the clouds
Letting me see the stars.

Gold

A frost or a wind
And they will be gone.
I have become used
To walking on gold.
A red carpet
Is nothing to this!

Tendrils

The same spirit
That pushes the bluebells
Through the bracken
Weaves tendrils between us
That surprise us in acts of love,
Sometimes from strangers.
The shock of tenderness is there.

The tender leaves of beech
And motion of water over
Brown stones where herons stand
Are no more precious than
The smile, the courtesy,
The kind word.

The soft sunlight through
The branches
Is not more warming
Than the candlelight
Illuminating the faces of our friends
As we break bread together.

Poems by Brooke Conklin

I grew up in Asheville, North Carolina, surrounded by some of the oldest mountains on earth. From these mountains, I directly experienced the unspoken knowingness built into all of nature. This knowingness has deepened my trust in the universe and myself. Learning to live from this space is a constant practice in my life. In nature I find a teacher, a companion, inspiration, solace, joy, patience, healing, adventure, and peace on this journey.

To connect with me further, please visit my YouTube channel, where I have some of my poems recorded in spoken word form.

A Walk into the Woods

A walk into the woods is like a walk into my soul.
Fallen leaves, like fallen dreams, trampled upon.
Gnarled and twisted branches,
like wounds that heal awkwardly,
grow into something disfigured.
Running water, like tears, flowing.
The deeper I travel the scarier it feels,
but the richer the rewards for daring to continue.
Sounds echo all around me.
The past, present, and future merge.
I am wrapped up in life, light, and love.
Fears melt away and expose a knowing that is infinite.
In this space of everything and nothing
is where all realms meet.
Join me here and experience peace,
even if only for a moment,
for in that moment you'll discover eternity is real.

Regrowth

Like a tree with strong roots and a stable yet flexible trunk, we can weather storms.
Sometimes limbs break and a part of us comes crashing down.
Usually these limbs are small twigs of distraction, but at times they are larger branches of anger, stress, or resentment that were fed too much and unknowingly grew too heavy.
When a storm breaks one of these branches,
it makes a noticeable change and provides a wondrous opportunity for regrowth.
If we can keep from getting in the way of ourselves too much, we'll find that we naturally grow toward the light.

Why?

Why do I wander through my thoughts like I wander through my life? No clear direction, just flowing until I hit a rock or shore or dam, where I stay momentarily stagnant until the force of life builds up enough oomph to push me on my way.

And why is it that, even if I see this is what will happen, my impatience builds? Is that impatience necessary?
Does it help to move me back into the flow more quickly?
Or does it add weight that holds me in that place longer?

I feel the pressure building again. I adjust to allow a bit more water to flow by me. It relieves the pressure just enough that I can go back to what I was doing. But the life force is building in me and soon the pressure comes back.

I adjust again and am once more granted a reprieve from the discomfort, but not as long this time.

The pressure soon returns. I'm becoming quite good at maneuvering around the pressure of life, but life is also learning. Eventually, small adjustments won't work.

I let go and life sweeps me into a new place, with new beauty and experiences to enjoy and learn from. But one day I notice that sinking feeling again, that pressure showing up again.

Really?
Wasn't I just free?
Can't life just leave me alone?

I don't want to move on. I'm tired of letting go, tired of taking leaps of faith, tired of being tired. I want to be able to stop without that nagging feeling creeping up, tugging on my shirt like a child desperately trying to get my attention.

Then I realize, it's me that is creating the stuckness.
It's me making the adjustments.
It's me freeing myself over and over again...
only to block myself later.

So why do I do this?
Why do I keep blocking?
Why does life have to flow around me?
Why can't life flow from me, through me?

Eleven Elements

Our bodies are made up almost entirely of eleven elements,
Six of which comprise 99% of our body.
99% - hydrogen, oxygen, carbon, nitrogen, calcium, phosphorus.

So what makes up our thoughts?
And why do we have them?
Self-discovery?

Perhaps as we evolve, we are discovering what all of us are.
We are each helping this universe to be aware of itself...
To realize and experience itself from within.

We are magic and majesty and eleven elements.

Poems by Andrea Buckle

I am a Human Givens Psychotherapist, a farmer, a mother of three, a happy adventurer, and a lover of life. After many years of leading, managing and coaching large diverse teams in the commercial sector, I returned to Wales and trained in Human Givens, a counselling modality that is non-intrusive and provides effective fast results.

I have a private therapy practice where I run sessions online or in local wellness centres. I love helping my clients achieve emotional balance and use guided visualisations of nature as part of their healing journey. I am passionate about helping people to become their best self by providing accessible effective therapy that allows them to live a life they love.

Alongside my therapy business, I work with my Dad on our family farm, breeding sheep and alpacas. I use our amazing alpacas for animal-assisted interventions and therapy, providing wellbeing sessions on the farm to enable people to experience natural calm. Being in the presence of alpacas and in the natural environment seems to melt away stress, reduce anxiety and re-centre people, enabling them to be in the present moment and allowing them to return to daily life, work, rest, therapy or rehabilitation with renewed happiness, calm and focus.

I live in beautiful rural Pembrokeshire under big skies far from everywhere, with my children, Kiran, Arun and Izzy, two cats, dog, giant snail and four bantam chickens. I am a country girl at heart and love animals and nature. I am fortunate to have chosen to live by the coast, near to where I grew up with access to many wonderful beaches and clifftop walks just a short distance from home.

Nature, especially the sea, is a powerful healer for me. This is where I give myself time for reflection and to pause from the busyness of everyday life, to walk, to breathe the fresh air and drink in the views.

Embrace Nature's Beauty

The stillness in the early morning light resonates
as I step through the dewy grass.

The quiet space inside of me is suddenly full to overflowing
as my senses drink in my surroundings.

A garden filled with colourful delights
as the sunrise basks everything in a golden glow.

The view towards the fields never-ending
as it rolls away with the hills.

The blackbird's song dances in the air
as it welcomes the new day, the new chapter.

I listen to the comforting familiar rustle of the leaves
as the wind plays in the trees.

My footsteps leave a damp path
as I embrace nature's beauty.

My Favourite Place

Newgale beach
Just within reach
Five minutes by car
Not very far
Golden sands
Beautiful lands
Meeting the sea
So gently
Walking here
Erases fear
Brings me calm
Nature's balm
Mind wanders
Time squandered
Such a treat
On two feet.

2023

L.G.

The Wild Leaky Sky

The wild leaky sky
Flinging possessions
With passionate abandon
Caused disruptive chaos
Batten down the hatches
Stay warm and dry
We can figure this out
In the calm after the storm
Just breathe and relax

Whispers of their Never-Ending Support

When I lost those I once held dear
A chink of my heart went missing too
So I lost myself in the world of my childhood –
Farmland, woods, beaches and many animals,

Found silence amongst trees, hidden paths and open fields,
Walked for miles on golden sands and beautiful cliff tops,
Foraged for feasts from nature's bounty,
Fed my family with my treasures.

My children walk the same paths with me
And our enchanted life is filled with love,
I am so blessed and grateful
To have found nature's healing power.

I sense their protection.
I know they surround me
The wind carries whispers of their never-ending support.

A Poem by Laura Copley

I work in the environment sector and nature for me is my happy place, the place I go to remind me who I really am; of who we really are as human beings–part of an incredibly awe-inspiring ecosystem–where there is no such thing as separation. I find comfort in that and in the therapeutic benefits of the natural world.

Willow

Compassionate rebel, radically rooting.
Determined in its resilience.
Weeping, as it leans into the waters of emotion.
Shimmering by the wind, free and with ease.

Determined in its resilience.
Ancient Goddess wisdom.
Shimmering by the wind, free and with ease.
A woven container to guide the heart.

Ancient Goddess wisdom.
A home where three children play, aligned to its meaning.
A woven container to guide the heart.
Giving in abundance, loyally supporting life's twists and turns.

A home where three children play, aligned to its meaning,
Weeping, as it leans into the waters of emotion.
Giving in abundance, loyally supporting life's twists and turns.
Determined in its resilience.

Poems by Claire de la Varre

I have worked as a therapist for over 15 years and have also undergone my own therapy to help me navigate challenging times. For me, the best therapy comes from going out into nature: climbing hills, walking by the sea, looking at the stars, and staring into crackling bonfires, accompanied by dogs, children, and friends.

I wrote my first poem at 11 and poetry continues to be a life-affirming pastime. I read and write poetry to help me work make sense of my thoughts, and recapture and process emotions past and present. Poems often come to me when I'm walking - there is something about the rhythmic movement that invites language to trickle, flow, or flood in... sometimes so fast that I am unable to capture the words or remember them long enough to get home and write them down.

I am fortunate to have lived in several different countries and traveled extensively over the past decade. Some of my poems reflect these experiences.

Yggdrasil Speaks

Oh, how you use us for your own ends!
You fail to comprehend the long span of time
that we grow into, standing still
and moving imperceptibly.

You spread out your picnic blankets,
let your babies play in our shade;
lovers pledge, widows cry,
men meet their deaths
at the end of a rope
or crucified on our branches.

You expect us to hold back Odysseus
from the Sirens, move raiders to other lands,
carry slaves across oceans.
And if you dared to lie awake at night
staring into the darkness,
you'd be unable to tell,
from the creaking and groaning,
which is more anguished -
wooden or human.

You lack understanding of our language,
you burn, slash, cut and carve us,
even as we house you, support you
when you eat and sleep,
provide both the conduit and the substrate
as your tiny thoughts flow,
pencil to paper.

You clog dance with leaden feet,
walk with wooden gait,
raise yourselves up and become stilted.

Your lives, printed on paper and framed,
your secrets hidden in drawers.

You stare into the flames, forgetting,
as we crackle into carbon and ash,
that you used us to beat eggs, children, and wives.

And in death you strip us of our unspeaking grace,
our sensual curves planed flat into boards and planks,
chopped, chipped, pulped, and splintered,
whittled and sanded in infinitely creative abuse.

Our steady, repetitive abilities purloined as you
apply those metaphors to your impossibly unrooted lives.
You bud, blossom, flower, and fruit;
turn over a new leaf.
Your banks borrow our branches.
You weep, like cherry and willow,
watched mutely by unblinking beech eyes.

Are you blind?
When you carve your birdhouses,
do you not see that we already shelter the birds?
Do you think you can breathe without us?
How long can you uproot and tear us down,
desecrate these long-suffering lands to feed
your ravening mouths?

Look around you!
Look around you at the wood... wood everywhere!
We died for you.

May shame stain your deciduous hearts.

2023

C.G.

Morning Thaw

Let's rise and watch the birds eating from the
wooden table under the bare rowan,
the seeds uncovered as the snow melts, haltingly.

All manner of small birds — robins, long-tailed tits,
finches, exposed in the staves of the tree
stark against the bitter white sky —
alight and eye the feast warily,
with jagged movement,
like a wink from a crystal
caught in an imagined sun,
darting down to snatch
sunflower, pumpkin, lentils, oats,
almonds and walnuts.
Almost the same as my own breakfast,
but tossed in butter,
a proffered defense to offset such chill air.

And now, the magpie, perfectly dressed for
this ashen season of iced monochrome,
makes its grand entrance,
brings its bold, disruptive presence
scattering songbirds as it descends to the table,
hops and pecks, towering above the small, metal animal sculptures
that you placed there
before the snow began,
so they could converse, unmoving,
in some language that birds do not speak.

A solitary crow, on the rooftop opposite,
pays no heed, preens its feathers,
effortlessly balanced on one leg,
eyeing the white distance.

Albatross

I came to New Zealand, with an albatross
hanging from my neck on a fine silver chain.
A man smiled at me... *Toroa!*
We are kindred spirits, you and I.

Out on Milford Sound,
on a perfect, late summer day,
as we neared the Tasman Sea,
there it was...
a lone albatross so high above
that we had no sense of perspective.

I stared and stared,
hand to my throat, touching
silver, until it had gone,
and I knew I could finally land.

Footfall

I walk, mid-afternoon, early August.
The air is thick, a presence, an obstacle
to confront or negotiate.

Dragonflies swoop and dart in pairs.
There is no wind.
The only air moving is that around me as I walk,
leaving trails of bubbling heat in my wake.

I listen.
Apart from my low, steady tread
I hear the thrum of distant traffic,
a plane fading away, crickets, birdsong.
A lone dog barks as if to defy the crush
of summer with the shatter of sound.

I hear
the clouds move,
the air shimmer,
a black-winged butterfly approach and retreat,
my heart twist and sigh, blood pulsing regardless,
feeling as though I have just woken
from a long sleep.

The silence wraps around me,
conspiratorial,
inviting me to shed my defenses,
open the conduit to the darkness
and speak my truth.

Mount John

My eyes shine, reflecting the numberless
stars of the tattered banner painted in a huge arc
across the heavens and revealed by darkness.
I gasp in delight as my lungs grumble
at the cold air, eyes following this Milky Way
into the deep unfathomable past.

The quiet, bumpy drive here, lit by
infrared and glow sticks; the anticipation
as we jostle, excited, in the minibus,
wrapped in our red Antarctica jackets,
warm breath condensing and fingers
slowly becoming chilled like dead stars.

We gaze through the telescopes
with dark-adapted eyes, as instructed,
see planets lined up to be dutifully inspected,
squint at the jewel box and the southern cross,
while the little child in my brain
tugging at the sleeve of memory
reminds me of the perfect joy of my first bonfire night,
holding baked potatoes with mittened hands
and painting the sky with sparklers.

And here we are,
staring at this treasure overhead…
such a common thing to our forebears,
trudging through their brief, dark lives,
and stolen from us by progress.
Oh, what a price we have paid for light!

But now I feel electricity
crackling and sparking nerve to nerve,
and who would have thought
that I would hear again
the calling of that icy, distant November
when I awakened from the dream of childhood
to a vast cold sense of belonging...
to the night, the past, the countless stars.

Under the Bridge

As I walked to work today
I looked around at the natural world and
the metaphors and lessons it held for me.

The water under the old stone bridge
sparkled so beautifully in the morning sun
that I almost cried.
Do not dwell on the past, however entrancing,
but cross the river and keep walking.

The weeds scattered along the side of the road
were dandelions, so brave and defiant,
waving brightly as I passed.
Pay attention to the small things along the way,
no matter how unimportant each may seem.

A blossoming branch
pushed over a high wooden fence
to make itself known,
brilliant against the faded blue sky.
Here I am again, world! Nature continues its
cycles of renewal and growth, regardless.

Loki The Dog

I miss him the most when the bracken is turning,
and I'm pushing through nettles and brambles,
up by the stane dyke, and the fence
with tufts of wool caught on the barbs.
I imagine I hear his hot breath, and see the
fireweed moving wildly in response to his
exuberant tunneling, tongue lolling in his joyous
open mouth, intent only on flushing out rabbits.

The rabbits themselves lolloped, fat, lazy,
and mostly unseen, in the other direction,
and although he careened after their fluffy white tails
he could only follow them as far as his head
would let him, which, happily for the rabbits,
was no more than three seconds or so.

By the burn, I remember his quivering, expectant gaze
as he waited for me to throw imaginary pebbles
into the peaty water, and permission to
hurl himself in, seeking something
forgotten seconds later.
His sleek seal head would emerge,
and he'd scramble up the bank, trailing cleavers.

My feet wet with dew, I breathe the mist
exchanged between Summer and Autumn
as they bicker over colour and texture.
I know that Autumn always wins.

I toss a single, solitary stone, and watch
the ripples of the past fade in the meandering burn.

When we were Turtles

If we were turtles... you were saying
And I smiled, but my mind drifted elsewhere,
Away from the group, and the conversation,
Captivated by a vision of the sunlit sea
above my head, moving with the water,
the green depths inviting me in...
Home. Like home. Almost home.

When we were turtles, we moved
with light and dark,
the eggs buried by moonlight,
hatchlings on their dark scramble across
the sand on the first day, this place that
would always pull us back,
before we felt the slap-slap of
the ocean, swell and hiss,
the tension between water and air,
between dive and breathe.

Ten thousand miles of water
to explore and remember.
Dreams sculpted by coral fingers,
sharks and hooks, fishermen's nets,
the moonlight streaked
on the wilderness of black sea,
the ambiguous invitations offered by
the endless open sky that turned and ticked,
as the days passed, unmeasured.

I remember when we were turtles.

A Poem by Cal Baker

This poem was inspired by Lucille Clifton's poem "won't you celebrate with me" and is sort of nature-ful!

Mountaintop

won't you celebrate with me? i'll send you an invitation, which i made out of crepe paper and purposefully spilled coffee on to stain it with sepia flowers. please, friend, join me at the top of this mountain where the air is crisp and seeps into your lungs in a way that sends happiness reeling in your chest. come with me and celebrate. paper lanterns decorate our patio of aspen roots and cobbles, which look like somebody spilled a messenger bag and forgot to pick the contents up again. the sky is clear, the layers of atmosphere like a skylight that lets in the sun but keeps the bad thoughts away. dream with me in the early morning, and we'll drink kava and watch the mice grow wings and flutter around like furred butterflies who grew fat feeding off their own self-praise. we'll celebrate you, and yourself, and me, and myself. we'll dance around wearing nothing but mosquito netting, which lets in the cold but makes us feel free. i liken it to skinny-dipping in the saffron sunrise, which makes the goose pimples on our skin feel just a tiny bit smaller and the warmth in our hearts feel ten times bigger. we might play backgammon if time allows. won't you come with me and celebrate?

Poems by Chris Horrill

I have spent decades working in East Africa, diving, surveying coral reefs, counting fish, setting up marine parks. I love nature deeply and I work to conserve it, yet I have experienced many examples of its traumas. My life's work has been to prevent and heal them. Perhaps I am a therapist of sorts... I wonder if I also feel that hurt. Just now I am a bewildered man in a dying world.

Man o' War

Every day I have a song.
Every day I talk to you in my head.
Different voices say different things.
At night it is quiet for a while,
then I wake, and sleep, and dream.

After the whirlpool,
I am floating in the hall of silver bubbles,
the only sound my breathing.
Above me, the silver surface of the sea,
below, serried ranks of fish in crevices,
facing where I have come from.
I am at peace.

I am thirty-five metres down,
Drifting along a cliff,
I turn slowly, fish- and coral-spotting.
Two eagle rays pass me.
The grace of their movement...
Big eyes and whip tails.

There is something on the surface,
Then there is pain.
Across my right cheek first,
then my forehead,
then my neck. Excruciating.
I can't see what it is, then I know.
I try to peel them off.

Whole

It is 3:30.
I am lying on my back
mentally examining the hole in my middle
that goes from just under the ribcage
into the pelvis.

Like André–I think that was his name–
when we found him, floating. Only birds
for company. Except that
I still have all my limbs, my genitals
and my face.
I know it is him because of the necklace,
wrapped around his vertebrae.
We carefully wrap him and take him.
I give the necklace to his mother and partner,
and try to say the right words,
as the pain takes them.

Why that image?
Why that memory as I dream?
The hole.
The loss.

Clients and Therapists

Poems by Felicity Jaffrey

Eustace, on his first trip to Narnia in The Voyage of the Dawn Treader, met a 'retired star.' Looking askance at the wise old man standing before him, he said, 'In our world, a star is a huge ball of flaming gas.' The star replied, 'Even in your world, my son, that is not what a star is but only what it is made of.'

The glory of nature is that it is so much more than the sum of its parts, nature surpasses its physical and biological components and is the manifestation of peace, adventure, meaning, story and metaphor. It is the handiwork, I believe, of a loving creator and has been entrusted to our care.

I am truly a nature lover and yet despite this I live in Cairo, a vast megacity and one of the world's most polluted. I love Cairo, but I don't always like it. It has become a place made of concrete and rebar and often gridlocked with fume-belching vehicles.

I work here as a Human Givens therapist. Sometimes when I ask clients to tell me of a special place that they can visualise as a place of serenity I realise that certain individuals have never experienced the 'peace of wild things' as Wendell Berry calls it. Most have never walked in a forest or gazed at fresh fallen snow. Some have seen the sea, but a sea enclosed by a hotel's parameters. Some have seen the desert, but a grim rocky roadside desert choked with plastic bags. Some have never run on grass or climbed a tree.

I hold the tension within me of a visceral longing to be immersed in nature - the wilder the better - and at the same time an exquisite gratitude that I am fortunate enough to have frequently bathed in the glory of mountains and forests and deserts and oceans. I don't take this lightly; I grieve for those unacquainted with such healing environments and for a developing world that encloses more and more people in concrete.

So I try my hardest to nurture nature wherever I live, to stand defiantly against fumes and fill the world with oxygen. I have made gardens on balconies and rooftops and small patches of unloved earth squeezed between unforgiving concrete walls.

I encourage my clients to find the trees that are here and marvel at them and notice them and befriend them. I invite them to climb up stairs and look up at the sky and notice the migratory birds that call in on their way from Africa to Europe and back again and to listen to their sweet song discerned beneath the city's monster roar.

I encourage them to grow herbs on windowsills, and keep plants on balconies, and I often give them cuttings to get them going such as the splendid local oregano plant which makes both Mediterranean pesto or middle eastern zaatar.

The secret to someone like me surviving in a place like this is both a grateful noticing and gentle tending of the nature that does live here, and this reveals another secret: that all of us need a grateful noticing and a gentle tending of the goodness within us.

Stubble

Each boot step is stubbed,
and it's not the clods:
later the plough will cleave
the sod and turn the cream-
brown earth to heave
in waves, laid out to breathe
and air-dry hard
to trip and break my stride.

But this is a softer stumble.
Stalks are shaved and
stick up straight - the stubble
stilts my gait and slows
my pace across the field
so I can gaze and breathe and yield.

2023   C.G.

Liber Abaci

Fibonacci nailed it.
His sequential spirals
magnifying in magnitude,
fractally fracturing,
point inwards and yet upwards.

A soaring symphony
of sunflower seeds
and dancing bees
bringing praise through
aggregating complexity
with its core built from
infinite simplicity.

The Ocean's Calling

A million billion trillion diamonds,
Outclassing Tiffany by infinity,
Dance at the point of consummation
Of sun and sea.
Each a perfect kiss
Reflecting, refracting, rejoicing
Again and again.

The steady pulsing of sun's life light
Perpetually marrying mesmerising movements
Of ocean odyssey.

Our sea breathes:
Bosom swell of parasympathetic deeps,
The curvature of waves,
And quickening of current and tide and wind.

There is purpose here,
An ancient and continual calling to
Embrace Earth,
Envelope us with patience and passion,
Surge story straight into our souls,
And surround us with peace.

Cairo

Crushing concrete,
Cruelly angular,
Creating corridors
Of swarming humanity.
Compressed and creeping
The combined stench and sweat of millions
Orphaned from earth.
Living and moving and having their being
In a city choked with chaos
"Where are you God?" said I,
"Lord of Creation, look at creation,
I can't see you!" said I.

There!
A space so narrow, unseen and pinched,
The smooth, grey, advertisement-studded
Trunk of a graceful palm
Gently growing,
Bursting out above roofs;
Wide, generous, gladsome branches
Swaying to the rhythm of a far more ancient beat,
Drinking in the sun,
Laughing with the sky.

And above the palm were doves,
Praising too in joyful play.
Perfectly attuned,
Silhouetted against the grey
Sun-scorched smog.
Suddenly a swift twist, a flash of white wings
And incandescent glory
There!
Even here, You are near.

A Popular Misconception about Fruit

That if you squish it, squash it, mash it, smash it,
Squeeze it, colour it, add additional smells to it,
Throw in chemicals and confine it to a
Carefully constructed tube
Designed to appeal to old people, young people,
Vain people, and health-obsessed people.
And you market it
Through the collective wisdom of
Boardroom people in suits or heels,
Each deliberately coated in other
Concoctions from other tubes,
And then arrange on shop shelves,
And sell it for something-ninety-nine,
That is obviously better than
Chomping a chunk of watermelon in the sun,
Letting the juice drip down your face,
Pretending you have a gigantic smiley mouth,
And spitting the pips away for fun.

Beneath the Bark

It's dark
beneath the bark
where the lice lark
about by parked
beetles.

2023

C.G.

The Dragonfly's Wedding

Infancy is tubular
And muddy.
Childhood parched
And crystalline.
Adolescence grows legs
And creeps around pond bottoms.

Growth in abundance,
Time of the essence,

Waiting for heavenly night lights to be right,
Strings of the wind to soar in delight,
Dawn to strike water as a bell so bright...

And the lovers arise,
Shimmering romance,
Orchestral poised passion,
'Til death do us part'
Above the font,
Glorying in life's purposes met on
This one sublime day,
To meet and to marry,
Cry, "freedom don't tarry"
Exult in the loving
Of dragonflies in May.

Plum Pits

Poor old plums,
So moist and plump and succulent,
Moisture beaded and full of ripe promise,
Scandalous purple, bursting with tart, sweet, goodness,
Hanging from trees like solid liquid drops of seduction.
Surely they don't deserve pits?

But yes, even plums have pits.
Not hairy, stubbly, deodorantly smeared pits.
Not receptacles of unwanted trash and Stig-dump treasured rusty
old bits pits.
Not despairing ghastly, endless, depressive pits.
Not even historical pits of elemental ice, wild beasts
and heroes.

But plum pits - hard brown, rough, crack-your-teeth-on pits,
Unwelcome as a chaperone on a date pits,
Make you think before you bite pits,
These pits have a special secret pit bit;
Did you know that plum pits have their own pits?
For hidden in the pit of the pit of the plum is a kernel,
And that kernel tastes of sweet almond.

Clients and Therapists

Poems by Liz Priestley

I grew up in Sussex, England, on the edge of Ashdown Forest, the real Hundred Acre Wood of A.A. Milne and Christopher Robin. When I was very young, I lived with a nanny who had cared for Milne's son.

I am now a corporate coach, hypnotherapist, yoga teacher and co-director of Elsewhere Small Group Travel with Claire de la Varre.

Where I Follow

I want to be on the other side of sad
over that hard wall that holds back happy
Stepping into the forest the rock falls away
back to the earth
Roots embrace the stone and a leafy hickory
bursts through the blackness
as if to say
I am here
Do you see me?
The fox trembles staring
His red fur fire in the glow of almost evening
And then he is gone
to that other place where I follow.

The Hundred Acre Wood

Dreams send me tumbling
down into that deep well of memories
and a small, outstretched hand
pulls me into the soft, green bracken
of the Hundred Acre Wood.

The air is full of songbirds
and lanky girls singing
an aria of melody and movement
We are taller in this summer season
Stronger in our muscles
all boney points and fluttering limbs
Knees scabbed, elbows battered
Friends bound through blood pacts
Fleeing mothers and rules
unfurling our fresh and powerful selves
blooming and breathing with the forest floor

We leap into damp and mossy
ditches through the curling ferns
that grasp and reach
around skinny ankles
Daring and wild we are
Children of the sixties
Exploding into our eleventh year
Drunk with our own magnificence.

Shiny new bicycles burst through
the yellow gorse and soar airborne
until the screech of brakes and
shrieks of joy shake the

primrose banks and startle rabbits
from their hidden places
Autumn creeps quietly into the wood
decay is spongy beneath our boots
We search for crawling, creepy things
Cool winds lift school skirts
Giggles leave us bent and breathless
Plaits and ponytails break free
and tangle with loosened ties
Girl warriors race through browning
fronds astride beloved steeds

Cold November sweeps the wood
Deer shiver and a wet brown blanket
lies where flowers and greenery grew
We walk with scarves wound tight
and buttoned coats
Our breath in plumes

The light of stars guides us home
still day by the old school clock
but dark comes early to the wood in winter
We peel away one by one
Running up garden paths to crackling fires
Mothers already apron-clad and stirring pots
of loving care

Christopher Robin walked our
ancient heath and withered witches too
Battle-scarred men and Royal Huntsmen
but they are nothing compared to
Five little girls forever young and bold and brave.

Clients and Therapists

Poems by Nancy Forer

Growing up beside farm fields bordered by forests brought nature and the turning seasons close.

Anticipating and appreciating the new awakenings at play were gifts for which I continue to be grateful.

Poetry is becoming shorthand for expressing experiences paralleling changes in my life with those I observe in nature.

My breath stole away...

When I rounded a columned corner of towering sandstone frozen in perpetual wait and wonder, the faint echo of those who traversed this same place reverberated in the silence of penetrating heat, giving me chills. I marveled at the manifestation of magic, mystery and miracle wedded before me.

Even stones thirst here, dreaming of rains to soak parched landscapes of endless summer. They swallowed, instead, ancestors' tears, wrung dry.

Clothed in coats of glorious colors, their rainbow ribbons splay across millenniums in gratitude that still shine up into the empty heavens.

To witness this, was to experience the profound, something touching on timeless sacredness - a holy communion between heaven and earth. I was (and remain) awed by the privilege and presence of the Divine made real.

What is it to die?

Mortal mantles melt away
the laughing dimples, frowns,
worry lines and wrinkles,
dissolving all traces of tracks the stitches could close
and those unreachable.

Pain, buried deeper than bones,
evaporates with them,
erasing all shades
of who we were and what we bore.

But left behind, kaleidoscope shadows
to fill in the empty
made whole again.

Transformation...
Becoming one
with all that was and is.

Now turned Holy.

Clients and Therapists

Poems by Christina Landers

Hello! I am a college student majoring in meteorology and material science engineering. My goal is to help the Earth in the ways of climate change and global animal extinction.

I am often described as a "witch" as I use the elements of the Earth for healing and daily use/meditation. I spend about 5-60 minutes a day having my "nature time."

Ever since the 6th grade, I have composed poetry. My family wished I would go into English to continue my poetry writing. I feel more inclined to help the Earth through science and I believe I will have more of an impact. I cannot count how many petitions I have signed in trying to help.

I love the world and its peaceful ways. It knows how to run, grow, and connect to the other life forms around it. It can be harsh and beautiful all at once. I feel as though we are merely visitors that have been allowed to live here rather than, "This is our world and we can do as we please."

I believe in nature's healing ways, and I want to show others it can heal them too.

I appreciate your time reading through my writing.

Full Moon Witch

sing us your song of the night
tell us your stories of the river
teach us to bleed dirt,
like you do.
tell us how to live with the animals.
show us how they persecuted you,
believing in the healing ways of the earth.
starlight woman
show me how to live in this world.

Modernism

lighting bugs are the flashlights of the night
blades of grass the carpet of the ground
trees provide us with shelter
birds, radio
we try to kill nature with our modern living
but it shapes the way we live
if only we would listen

Twilight

the soft night quiets the mind.
the breeze blowing the curtains,
through the open window.
crickets chirping their lullaby,
for the babies next door.
I wish I could escape into the darkness
the moon calls my name.
my dreams running wild like the untamed wolves,
the constellation guiding their way.
shifty fox, navigate me through the forest.
show me how to be in the twilight.
let me live in your undomesticated world,
dozing in the sunlight.
teach me how to be wild,
how to live,
how to be.

Poems by Shelley Enarson

I am a writer living in Durham, North Carolina. My work has been published in The Chicago Reporter, ColorLines and Insight Magazine. I grew up overseas and spent seven years as a humanitarian storyteller living in East Africa, working on pan-African palliative care policies. I find nature to be an immersive source of solace, wonder, and courage in my journey through complicated grief.

2023

C.G.

An Immigrant's Pinchers

Each time I moved –

I thought I could shrink, small
contained like a shell

huddled between sand, light and sea

it started when tide after tide
changed my shorelines

while I burrowed my rigid spine in the earth
trying to blend, curve and never move, again

waiting to be gathered
rather than to gather, myself.

What I found was this--

Though sand shape-shifts to tender toes,
it was never meant to keep small shells in place.

And with time, I became more hermit crab -
than shell
probing, pinching, groping

my way to break new turf
in white foaming waves

So forgive me for being rough against my ridges
It's grit that has tethered my roots.

We were like animals

Claws   drawn
jaws   clenched
yanking hair
bite of words
raised voices   raised power
really, screeches of weakness

we were prey
while we prayed
pleading restrain   from one another

our rise and fall – missing umpires
no mother—no father
to stand in our way,   as sisters.

Until one of us,
until I would run
fast   as fire

can spread
to open spaces

where
I am
still roaming.

We were like animals.
what we have now
is shedding fur
as sisters do when losing
their pack.

When snow collapsed

When snow collapsed
     like a blanket
          of wild promises
               I stood, straddled
               between time and place

Snow tricked us
     through the cold air beneath us
          allowing softness between us
               when we paused at its wonder

In December, it fell
     to tell us, compel us
          to stop spinning our wheels
               and trade traction
               for play.

Clients and Therapists

A Poem by Alistair Humphrey

I am a Public Health Physician and Family Doctor living in New Zealand. I was born in Edinburgh and raised in London but my work has taken me from the jungles of Central America to the outback of Australia; from the council estates of England to the megacities of Asia; from the frozen steppes of Mongolia to the balmy shores of South Pacific islands. I ride a bike wherever I can and take my guitar which I play with prolific mediocrity.

There is a well-known Māori whakatauki (proverb):

He aha te mea nui o te ao?
[What is the most important thing in the world?]
He Tāngata! He Tāngata! He Tāngata!
[It is people! It is people! It is people!]

The planet is becoming overwhelmed with humans and their livestock, which now constitute 96% of the mammalian biomass of the planet. Small island developing states, such as Kiribati, are running out of room while the population continues to grow and rising sea-levels shrink the contaminated land the people are crowded into.

Perhaps it is time to change the proverb to:

He aha te mate o te ao?
[What will kill the world?]
He Tāngata! He Tāngata! He Tāngata!
[It is people! It is people! It is people!]

He tāngata, he tāngata, he tāngata.

The waves that crash over the reef
Are Gaia's tears -
Pouring out her grief, but no one hears.
Ssh. Ssh. Ssh. Ssh.

The trade winds breathing through the trees
Are Gaia's sighs.
She fears the rising seas – her coral dies.
Aah. Aah. Aah. Aah.

The soft, white sands under the palms
Are Gaia's hands –
They sink beneath the plastic, glass and cans.
Krr. Krr. Krr. Krr.

Warfare, refugees and poverty,
As Gaia knows,
Are driven as the population grows.
Waah! Waah! Waah! Waah!

It's the elephant – not the room;
It's the booming – not the boomers;
It's not the generation – it's the generating;
It's not the carbon – it's the footprint;

It's not the rising sea or CO_2
As Gaia pleads
Repeatedly, "It's nothing new –
It's you.   It's you.   It's you.   It's you."

~ Tarawa, 2023

A Poem by A. K. Olsen

Naturally Aligned

As the Taoist *sits – in* this... Now
So the flower blooms.

As the Painter *feels* what scenery speaks,
So the lighting arises and falls...
like a metronome's arm slicing to-and-fro.

Birdsongs elicit... attention – when heard.

Color and hue alight like a butterfly
on that which we *think* we *see*.

The Quanta Leap and so do *we*
as heart-to-heart we *be* as the Bee,
who moves as if by intuition and
sensory awareness, and yet...
through *the hive mentality*,
can each be here-now,
and over-there, too?

Where is your attention now?
On this, or that?

What reality do you want to create?
Set A or Set B?
Where is the power?

What is magical in garden spaces
and beautiful places?

Where are you locating yourself
in-between sun-and-moon, today?

If you are on the Equator?
If you are on one or the other Axis Points?

Do principles, premises,
and cognitive processes consume you?
Or, at a moment's notice
do you *open* to *awe*, *inspiration*, and *curiosity*...
when squirrels and otters seem to play?

How does *observer-created reality* impact you--
when *nature* appears *live* and
Moving in your field,
or on your shared path?

Are *you* the one who is
Deer-in-the-Headlights?
Bees on the Move?
Dragonflies on your Toes?

Is your moment-to-moment attention
open to the rhizomatic entry and exit of *nature* –
or, is that an illusion?

What is your *nature* when you are
naturally sitting *in*...
the Now?

Clients and Therapists

Poems by Jennifer McInroy

Nature has always been a part of me. It brought blissful happiness when I was a child. It uplifts and helps me breathe when I am stressed. In the saddest moments of my life, it sat with me and gave comfort, and brought a smile back to my face.

When I am immersed in nature, I feel like I belong and even when I'm not physically there, I get a powerful connection to a deeper meaning of life when I imagine or remember experiences during the process of writing poetry.

It has been a few months that I have been writing as a way for me to switch off from stresses that can feel overwhelming. It's a positive action I can focus my mind on, no matter where I am. And it makes me more present and engaged as I collect words and experiences day to day that I can play with later; it's like solving a puzzle. Finding a natural rhythm and using simple rhymes feels soothing to me, there are no surprises!

Ultimately, I hope that my words might bring a sense of peace or joy to others having a difficult time and remind them they are not alone.

A Message from Nature

I wait for you beyond the silence,
I empower you to find true sense,
I ground you to calmness and kindness,
I bring honesty and acceptance.

I restore meanings and connections,
I resonate beauty and pleasance,
I help you find the silver linings,
I wait for you beyond the silence.

Wherever the Answers Lie

See emotions reflected in the sky,
Choose what serves and let others drift on by.

Feel the biting air, fresh breeze on your skin,
Notice how it stirs up power within.

Watch the swirling, ripples in the water,
That nourish and nurture when you falter.

Walk or run, pound the earth below your feet,
Strength rises up, now there is no defeat.

Wise old trees, rustling leaves a reminder,
This moment will pass, won't last forever.

Birds fly by, uplifting echoes they call,
It's a miracle we are here at all.

Cairngorms

The magical mists
On the landscape, drifts
Of snow melting to rain.
Down the hills
The water fills
To the river's gain.

Atop the cairn, ice rifts
Hang on, white kissed
A glacier hides the hare.
An eagle thrills,
The ptarmigan stills,
Absorbed we stop and stare.

Hello

My name is nature, I am here for you,
Do you remember me in plants that grew
Around your home or favourite parks walked through?
In fields of daisies and cows watching you.

The blackbird singing from the rowan tree,
I become your soul and set your heart free,
Thoughts locked within but I can be the key,
When you feel lonely, reconnect with me.

I am the bee, the mouse, the fox, the deer,
When you need comfort, I am always near,
Reach up to the sky and let go of fear,
Look for the clouds to wonder and hold dear.

Recognise my love in the flowers' bloom,
Sad to be gone, yet will meet again soon,
I'm between the stars and the cratered moon,
The crow that caws when the clock passes noon.

The otter, the bat, the beaver the stoat,
I'm your life jacket to keep you afloat.
One day at a time, seek hills so remote,
Time to breathe, feel at ease - get on your coat!

Hope

How can it have been yet another year?
Nights are getting light, yellow gorse is here,
Returning ospreys and swallows are near,
Look out for bees and butterflies to cheer.

Daffodils shift and shimmy in the breeze,
Sweet scented blossom bloom on the trees,
Whispers of secrets weep from the willow,
Rushing the river, reassures, overflows.

Leaving behind the grey skies and wallow,
Through fresh fields of yellow you must follow,
Ferns unfurling, the summer is calling,
Enjoy the beauty today, no stalling.

2023

C.G.

Castle Campbell

It was one day at Castle Gloom,
We met a barn owl, rusty broon,
Eyes tight shut but followed us 'roon,
Still sleeping at dusk, awaiting the moon.

Another day at Castle Campbell,
I saw a mouse dart in the bramble,
A moment's awe breaks up my ramble,
Under the oaks all crooked and mangled.

A starry night in Dollar Glen,
To find a badger in its den,
They spot a hedgehog 'mang the fern,
Bats click and swoop, catch moths 'roon them.

A fresh dewy morning, the wildflowers I follow,
Down to Burn of Care where it meets Burn of Sorrow,
And soaring on high I watch swifts or swallows,
I promise myself I'll come back tomorrow.

A Poem by Drew Lesslie

My name is Drew Lesslie and I am a Musician and Songwriter from Glasgow, Scotland.

I have always found language to be fascinating and I believe that complex concepts and feelings can be explained with surprisingly simple words when used in the right context.

Since I was recently diagnosed with Adult ADHD, I have found solace in lyric writing and poetry, using words as a vehicle to express my thoughts, process my emotions, and come to terms with my new reality.

'The Dragonfly' is a reflection on some of my feelings around my recent diagnosis, and other recent sizeable changes in my life. Coming to terms with massive change has made me realise that the life I imagined and prepared for throughout my childhood and adolescence doesn't really exist, and the reality of living is much less clear than we are taught while growing up.

This poem is one of mourning and longing but writing it has helped me accept the change in my life and move forward with new positivity and gratitude for things I have yet to discover.

2023

L.G.

The Dragonfly

Lifelong preparations to take first flight,
Cast off old skin and reveal my true might.
No more a nymph, stalking in the shadows
Freedom found not far above the shallows.

Wings unfold, expand and blood pumps through
An empty cocoon, leave all that I once knew.
Escape this prison, take off to the sky,
I'm gifted purpose, I must learn to fly.

I find kindred souls; one, two, twenty,
Yet things above the surface seem empty.
Nothing like my imagined lucid dreams,
New life is less exciting than it seems.

I flit around, a pointless pretty pest,
A pretty pointless existence, I jest.
I'm longing for the depths, as King I ruled,
This evolution doesn't have me fooled.

Once I was a predatory master,
Now time passes, ever, ever faster.
I have no purpose, merely passing days,
I long for a return to those old ways.

Take me back to the water of my youth,
The river ever flowing, my real truth.
Take me back, to the water I belong,
That gentle brook that used to be my home.

Take me back to the water.

Poems by Dorothy Baird

I live on the edge of Edinburgh where I work as a psychotherapist and lead occasional writing groups in the community. I have three grown up children.

My poetry has been widely published in magazines and I have two collections of poetry. Leaving the Nest, my first collection, was published by Two Ravens Press. Mind the Gap, my second collection, was published by Indigo Dreams Publishing.

Subtraction of Grief was first published online in Ink Sweat & Tears webzine. Leaning was commended in the Autumn Voices Competition 2022.

Morning was published online as part of the University of Plymouth and Nottingham Trent University Covid archive. https://poetryandcovidarchive.com/

Dear Mother, this is snow

The sky has torn itself
into whirling scraps
or it's a goose
shaking its feathers,
or fragments of amnesia
remembered and spilling back
into space – I don't know,
they call it snow
and snow goes white
and blurring, snow goes
smudging lines and rubbing
out the football pitch,
people's hats, the cars,
all white and soft, and feet print
new words on these strange pages.
It's water on my tongue, and
in my hand, so cold –
did I mention it's cold, mother?
It's a taste of metal, a shiver,
a hand-packed snow-stone
arcing through a swan feathery sky
to splodge
on a jacket or a tree, its hush
a shoosh,
a stillness like a baby sleeping.

Horgabost

A gale force wind
wrestles all night with our tent,
tugging guy ropes and pegs,
whipping its poles, snapping
the flap of nylon, as if
determined to wrest it
from the grass and blast it ,
over the white sands
towards Beinn Dhubh
like a belle-dressed ghost
or a Hebridean angel
jangling Celtic death songs
in the ropes of its lyre.

Badger Watch

It wasn't so much the badgers
I'll remember, though their shadowy
forms caught my breath
as they rustled in the earth mounds

and nosed in twigs and bluebells - no,
it was rather the waiting,
the five of us, faithful
to the silence we'd agreed on,

crouched downwind, while night
eased itself among the trees
and sheep coughed in distant fields,
when we learned the language

of each other's face; how
in the sweeping dark
we dwindle to a beating heart,
and how in the long emptiness,

the sliver of hope still rises.

Rumbling Bridge

I have been thinking about how the river
  slides and rolls between these rocks for ever,
   and how its thick snake

slithers through stone
  on the same journey
   and always new,

winding from some spot
  in far away grass, where
   flies dance not knowing

how this spurt or seep of wet
  will end, and not, I'm sure,
   caring much either,

preferring to stitch the air
  with their crazy pattern
   and be gone. I think

I will always think
  about things. But how
   would it be,

just for once, to dance
  or slide
   into the next moment

and let go of everything
  - except the soft eddy of air,
   the long resistance of stone?

Autumn

It's the dying season,
though *dyeing* is more fitting
for the golds and yellows and browns
that soak into the leaves

and wash the hills
and the loch-side with
a maelstrom of reds,
and when the sun shines

no stained-glass window
ever glowed
like the copper beech
at the bottom of our garden: so

this death is
not a simple thing
- and whether or not
you have ever stopped to ask,

the darkness of the earth
still holds in its closed mouth
the old washerwoman's secrets
of a green spring.

Filling the Well

Sometimes the day comes
when you have given everything
in your attempts to be everything
to everyone. You will know this day
when your small bird cannot flex
its wings against the wind,
when your sun cannot heave itself
over the horizon, when you lower
your bucket into the well and hear it
thud against the clay.

When this day comes you must take off
the smile that is no longer truly yours,
and batten down your heart
that now betrays you with its giving.
You must hold your hands
about your ears, for their voices
are the siren calls that will bind you
to them. And you must walk or limp or run
through the door you can barely see,
into the darkness of a lonely room,
into the ocean of an empty moor,
into the wide arms of the forest,

and sit or walk until from deep within
a trembling starts to pulse,
and your diviner's hands sense
what the oak tree and the sycamore
and the worm that flicks its tail
as it bellies into the earth

all know: the source
is the same source
you are thirsting for. Drink deeply.
Be still. Be slow. The world can find its way

without you. For you must drink
until your well is filled, until your feathers
plump, until a new sun rises
in the winter of your eyes. Then,
and only then, may you return,
and when they see you, lush
against the light, let them
stand back a little further than before
and be amazed.

Leaning

She needs to lean on birdsong these days.
And on the evening' smells of silage
from the fields, the warmth of day
dissipating, as earth adjusts
to the arriving dark: *the gloaming.*

She leans on that word, too.
With its gloom and its loam
and its blossom, fading
but still white and myriad
on the solid strengths of the trees.

All these are pillars of her days.
Her foundation and her refuge. Where else
has anyone found support
in strange times?

At night, awake to the silence
of her house, she hears the wind
in the birch trees and the blackbird
beginning to think about dawn
and finds solace
in its unfailing instinct to sing.

Solace is another word she likes.
Sol and ace. So and lace. The so lace
of the blossom trees is tatted
by something bigger than she is,
bigger than darkness is. And turning
her pillow over to a cool spot, she leans
on that too.

Morning

He is heavy with morning. As if its weight
has flattened him and drained all his rivers.
He stays in his dressing gown.

She says, 'Let the countryside go for a walk
inside you. Let the skylark rise and rise
inside you. Turn yourself inside out
then in again, but bring the foundlings
of Black Hill and Capelaw, the rolling heather,
the yellow stars of celandines to light
your gloom. She pauses for breath.

You've got sky from your window, she says,
learn to love the sky. It's enough for
the skylark and the swift. It'll do you too,
till your feet find the ground again. Sit
by the window and get to know the light.

And if you need to, weep. Weep until all your tears
have flowed. Empty yourself like the clouds
release their rain. Pour your sadness into the day.
It is big enough to hold it.

When you're all wept out, you'll be washed
like the coloured saris in the Ganges are laid out
on the shores to dry. Give yourself time.

The day will tiptoe back into you, whispering
endearments, beckoning. Follow it. Follow it

into the white blossoming on bare trees
into the shades of green behind
the tulips, into the heron still and sharp
in the river. Into the absolute second
of existence. You're alive. Now
what is it you can do?

Either Here or There

There is a way of walking by the reservoir
when there is only the water's wingbeats
against the shore and the hills
in their shifting colours, the wrinkled light
of mud furrowed by bike tracks and the wind
through the railings, moaning
like ghost-breath over bottle tops.
And there's another way when the path
just carries you – and the hills and the water
dissolve into conversations you wish you
hadn't had and thoughts about deadlines
and bills and the leaky roof, and suddenly
you're back at the car
an hour older.

Subtraction of Grief

Yesterday I slipped into a broken space
the wind couldn't mend. Beside me the reservoir
dazzled in the cold sunshine and larch trees
losing their copper needles in the fleecing gusts
were still, are always, all one in themselves, needing
nothing but wide light and earth and rain.
I know we, too, can be all one in ourselves -
we can walk in the sound of the stone-chat
and sense the certainty, the rightness of things -
but a flash of memory out of the blue or the grey
can render us aching and minus -
and we don't even know what it was
in the water's light or the rasp of a crow
or the curling edges of a fly-agaric, kicked over
in a hiding of grass, that cut through the one
we were, to make the wound smart
as if a salt fingerprint rubbed our past
into the present and we're raw again
and lonely as only love can make us.

Clients and Therapists

A Poem by Àstrid Heilmann

Born in Rio de Janeiro, Brazil, on a Thursday with a full moon and rough seas, to a German father and a Swiss mother, Àstrid simultaneously learned to speak German and Portuguese.

Holidays, frequently spent with the family on a farm high up in the Serra da Mantiqueira mountain range in the state of Minas Gerais, have marked her the most. Long stays allowed for close contact with nature. Happy childhood and adolescent memories include horseback rides, waterfall showers, contemplation of ants transporting leaves, puddles filled with tadpoles, frogs croaking at night, hummingbirds, butterflies, a range of interesting insects and, of course, multicolored and fragrant flowers! Strong roots were then formed with this area.

While switching careers from systems analyst to psychotherapist, the poet was born and her first poem, 'Sansara', came to be. Ever since, inspiration has visited without a warning, sometimes waking her up in the middle of the night with the urge to write.

Leaving behind eight years of work at a clinic in Rio de Janeiro, Àstrid moved to the same mountain range area of the farm of her youth. São Lourenço has eight medicinal springs located in a beautiful park with lake and abundant flora and fauna. It is the perfect place to seek poetic inspiration. 'Here is home!'

Actually, it was right here, that Àstrid and a majestic yellow Ipê tree met. Every winter she visits the tree that inspired this poem. Yes! Ipê trees bloom in wintertime, bringing a message of hope that soon a new cycle will start in the spring.

This is how Àstrid's first publication, 'Cycles', was born, released in September 2023. It's an illustrated poem about the cyclical nature of evolution.

Ipê

Look! Such a beautiful ipê!
Ahh... I love ipê trees!
They bloom in all colors,
The colors of the rainbow,
And my heart beats happily.

The flowers and their scent
transport us to this sublime moment.
Flowers and their fragrance
that nourish love.
Flowers are praise
from Mother Earth to God
in this world of trials and duty.

So, let's enjoy the flowers
and their colors.
Let's breathe deep of their scent
until... full contemplation
in gratitude sets in,
and finally cures all pain.

Ipê

(Original Portuguese Version)

Ipê... vê que lindo Ipê!!!
Ahhh.... Eu amo os ipês!!
Tem de todas as cores...
Cores do arco ... *Íris*
Meu coração faz bater feliz

Ahhhh, as flores com sua fragrância,
nos transportam a sublime instância!
Flores e seus odores
que alimentam os amores.
Flores são louvores da Mãe Terra a Deus
no globo das provas e expiação.

Então...
espiemos as flores
com suas cores.
Respiremos fundo seus odores!
até que se instaure ...
plena contemplação
de gratidão que por fim, ...
curará todas as dores

A Prose Poem by Helen Percy

As a hill shepherd in the Scottish Highlands, the rhythms of birth, death, and rebirth are part of everyday life. Reflected in the changing of the seasons, they are imprinted in my being.

I've always looked to the mountains and the clouds to revive my spirit and am so fortunate to have wild places at my door. However, when my sheepdog, Goose, was stolen, and died from injuries inflicted by the thief, I was devastated.

The bond between a shepherd and a dog can be extraordinary. I sought help from a therapist in coming to terms with the cruelty of Goose's final months, and the evil intent of his captor.

I. A Cruel Tormentor

She promised to return Goose to me. Repeatedly, she reneges on her word. Months pass, and I miss him more rather than less. Every morning, I long to be greeted with his enthusiastic solo: 'Owo owo woooo!'

I spend Christmas feeling miserable. There is a tight knot underneath my diaphragm, and I fall to sobbing. I know she is avoiding my calls and is plotting to withhold my dog forever.

The young woman to whom I entrusted my most precious companion is taunting me. I beg her to let me see my dog. I struggle through another fortnight, another month, another season, hoping next time she will bring him.

Her behaviour is treacherous. By now she has retained Goose long beyond the extent of our agreement. This spoilt young madam thinks it fine to steal my dog from me, because she has always had whatever she wanted. Besides, her boyfriend is a gamekeeper: he has half a dozen spaniels and retrievers. She still has her own collie, too. The lovebirds have each other: why must they hold on to my dog?

For months, I have hidden from her my anxiety about Goose. I have maintained a policy of politeness and patience, even when I realise she is keeping Goose from me deliberately. She has never given me her boyfriend's address, and I think the best hope I have of seeing Goose again is to 'play it cool', despite every broken avowal.

It is exactly when I drop my guard and plead with her to let me see him, in a brief message admitting, 'I have this dread that I may never see him again,' that she spies my weakness and moves in for the kill. Her instant reply is, *'NO. I am not willing to part with him.'*

How can she do this? He is MY dog! He was the yawning bundle that I held in my arms as a puppy and spent so much time training to help me herd sheep. He is my own treasured Goose, who has worked for me loyally for almost a decade.

II. Necromancer

She is the green-bottle fly: in the hot summer sun, she seeks out a host on which to lay her thousand tiny eggs. She hones in on my wound, and she will buzz around me as I suffer, like a sick ewe holed up in the bracken.

I can throw back my head in irritation, but time and again the fly lands on the festering sore. She will not desist until she has emptied herself of her vile progeny. Satisfied, her evil ovaries emptied, her legacy becomes a seething mass of flesh-eating maggots that burrow under skin. They are necromancers. Boring deep into a living hors d'oeuvre, they produce a grey slime of putrefaction; they poison, ingest, grow fat: within days they have a cadaver as their main feast.

How could I have failed to observe the green sheen on her thorax? When she took Goose away from me, she laid her yellow-orange eggs. From the point that she saw how much damage they would do, she became gleeful.

Goose is on my mind every minute of every day, and most of the minutes of every night too, since I hardly sleep. At my core is a void. I feel sick. I have to remind myself to breathe.

'*You can't have loved him that much if you gave him away*' she goads. Gave him away? Goose? There is no way on earth I would have "given" up my beloved dog, for someone else to decide I could never see him again. That would have been akin to chopping off my arm and tossing it away. These last six months it has felt just like that – as if a limb has been severed. With her each successive unkept promise to return Goose, I have become more fretful for his well-being.

Years ago, Goose set out across Scotland to find me. That time, I'd left him with a friend only for a few days, but he'd scaled a high deer fence. Can I will him to escape again now, and find his way to me? He is older, sleepier, less agile.... He could be injured, hit by a car, encounter untold hazards.... No, I must not hope for him to do this. This time I am the one who must set out to find him.

When I do, I'll wish I had the courage to stand up to the manipulative bully that she is; not for what she has done to me, but because she is breaking Goose's heart.

This little diva knows she has taken not only my soulmate, but also the most essential tool of my trade, as I cannot earn my living as a shepherd without my star of a sheepdog.

'How can she do this?' I keen, over and over again. *'WHY would she?'* Soon the reason becomes apparent: she will hold Goose to ransom…. She demands £2,000.

III. Two Thousand Pounds!

Friends and neighbours start a crowd-funding campaign to raise the money, and it is through this that two people from her work convey that she has kicked Goose repeatedly…

Her extortion complete, my friend Jane offers to transfer Goose to me. We meet in a carpark. When I open Jane's car door, Goose is curled on the passenger seat. I crouch down and speak his name quietly. He raises his head, hesitates, and then licks my nose. Tears fall from my cheeks onto his dark fur.

Goose is subdued. Bewildered. There is an immense, palpable sadness about him. It is as if he believes he has been brought here for a few minutes. This is a fleeting, final tryst, so that he can say farewell. Why else is everyone here weeping?

I coax him to out of the vehicle to let me make a fuss of him. Now, he does roll onto his back and invite me to rub his belly; but it is not with the unbounded joy I expect. He does not leap out and run around in excited circles, wagging his tail. He thinks he will be taken back to her house and will never see me again.

Jane, sensitive to his anxiety, starts her engine: *'I'll go now, so Goose realises I'm not going to take him away again.'*

I make much of him for a few minutes after Jane has left, then I open the door of my own van. I invite him to come with me. Goose remains motionless. He believes he is going to be left here, on his own, in the middle of the parking area. He is resigned to this desertion.

He must make his own way now; but he does not know where he is supposed to go. All he understands is that from now on he will be alone. No-one will care for him or meet his needs.

My heart is breaking for him. I am swallowing back salt tears. My Goose, my Goose... My poor, beautiful boy.

Goose is tense during the short journey home, his eyes full of worry. We pull up in the yard at the cottage and he half-stumbles from the foot-well. He seems dazed, as if part of his mind is in a wilderness. He reminds me of a friend I visited in an asylum once, who'd been drugged into a state of numbness and did not know where he was.

There is a thick mist wrapping itself around Goose. He dallies along the path as if he is in a fog; a confusing dream. Once inside the cottage he lies down in a corner. He's not sleeping, but he's wiped out. He is flat; unable to respond emotionally.

I am howling now. How could she? How could anyone do this, to any animal... let alone to my compliant, obedient Goose, who would give all he had, until his little heart burst with the effort?

Her behaviour has been hideous, despicable, and mercenary. There are many things a sensitive dog can comprehend. The twisted and duplicitous behaviour of flawed human beings, however, is beyond him.

IV. Goose is Home

The blossom-laden lilac-tree is rich against a background of boiling pewter clouds. Red-roan cows tear up fresh clover noisily, with yard-long tongues.

The April-born lambs are growing apace and need to be brought into the sheep fank for earmarking and vaccinations.

Goose brings in droves of ewes with their bouncing offspring. He streaks back and forth to funnel them down to the river-crossing.

After the first morning's gather he is tired, and so I leave him sleeping in his armchair while I work in the pens. An hour later he is still sleeping, but when I walk through the garden gate at dinnertime, I can hear him crying desolately inside the cottage. In the past he did not mind being left alone, but there must be some residual insecurity since his being held hostage. He has nightmares about desertion, and I vow I shall always make him a bed where he can see or hear me.

The second and third days, once his part of the job is over, he snoozes in the low-sided basket on the back of the quad bike. He is content and fulfilled. Dosing there, he knows I cannot go anywhere without him.

On the fourth morning, Goose is sitting at the foot of the steps into the tractor shed while I set up some gates. When I am ready, he stands up, twists round to follow me, and screams out as if he has been struck by an arrow.

I try to soothe him. He stops shrieking, but walks with his back arched up, as high as a ferret. He is dragging his back end along in the dust behind him. He has no feeling in his back feet. He cannot even wag his tail.

A part of Goose's spinal structure has split. Her kicks have been severe. The local vet examines his x-rays and says, without conviction, that if I take him to the big animal hospital, there's the slenderest chance that surgery may be attempted.

Can I transport him all the way to the city, in this much pain? Then abandon him with strangers? Since his ordeal Goose howls with anxiety if he wakes up and I am not in the room beside him.

Even if he survived an operation, at the very best he might learn to walk again. After months as a paraplegic, he could, possibly, draw himself stiffly and painfully across the farmyard.

Would that be any kind of life for a creature who once sped away to flank the straying ewes, ran races in the meadow, and leapt fences for the sheer joy of flying? Never again would he trot ahead of me to chaperone the sun-glossed cattle to late-lush pastures, nor accompany me to the frosted slopes to feed the winter sheep.

I ask for him to be injected with painkillers, and for his bladder to be emptied to make him comfortable.

I want to take him home for one final night. I covet this time, to say goodbye to my dog and to thank him for all he has given me. Then he will be put to sleep, in his familiar environment, while I stroke his neck.

I am inconsolable in my self-blame for having failed to protect Goose from her writhing maggots. In these last hours, at least, I can do my best for him. I can give him a quiet place to rest. I can promise that his suffering will not be protracted.

V. Vigil

We have one last night and one last day to be together. I set a mattress on the floor and make my own bed there under the kitchen table with him, where I can lean the crown of my head against his chest.

'*You're a good Goose,*' I murmur. His neck is damp from my tears.

Goose is drowsy. His paws and shoulders twitch. I hope he is dreaming of bringing down the ewes from the heathered hill; of trotting through galaxies of orange-gold asphodel above the shining loch.

'*I love you, Goose. I just love you!*' I breathe.

I've spoken those words to him a dozen times a day since I ransomed him from her. I think he is too deep in drug-induced sleep to hear me repeat them now, but he opens his eyes and cocks one velvety ear towards me. The muscles at the sides of his face twitch. He pulls back his black gums at the corners of his mouth and affords me his special flickering smile.

I do not leave his side for the whole night. Nor, except to let out the ducks, the following day. He seems peaceful. I hold back my sobbing, in order not to disturb him; but it feels as if my own heart is about to stop, too. I wish we could leave together, and neither one of us has to bear this Great Parting.

I have had Goose back with me for just five weeks. Not to have had this short, precious time, and had not to have known how death greeted him, would have been unendurable.

The vet is here now and has attached the line through which runs the liquid that will still his pulse. Goose raises his head. In this last minute of his life, his wide eyes fill with apprehensiveness, and fix on mine. He seeks my bidding, as always he has done: *'Where shall I find the flock? Whither should I guide them?'*

O Goose! My Goose! You must run to a far distant hill. Be fleet, and do not look back, because I cannot follow you there. Your broken body no longer carries you, but you will have no more need of it, I promise.

Race, loyal dog! Run free across the moorland, where the bog-cotton and the grass-of-Parnassus blow like snowflakes in the wind, and where the stonechat and the meadow pipit chant merrily. Go swiftly now, my faithful one.

VI. Morning

I spend a second night on the floor beside Goose.
His eyes are still dark and shining, like newly opened chestnuts; but his ribcage no longer rises and falls.

Almost midsummer, the hours of darkness are scant.

I drag myself away from my vigil sometime between three and four o'clock. Tightening my bootlaces resolutely, I lift a spade from the woodshed, and set out.

Gravedigger, mourner, pallbearer, priest.

The sky is pink.

Across the moor, the cry of the curlew burbles up, as water from the purest mountain spring. At its zenith, its aria pierces the veil between earth and heaven. The cadence falls away with the melancholy of a requiem.

In between birth and death,
there is such a short time for singing.

VII. Epilogue

Swallows congregate on their end-of-summer trapeze
Leaf-fall is followed by frost
Next the hawthorn is laden with blossom
Now the copper-coloured adder basks on sun-warmed stone

Grief is the deserted nest a meadow-pipit made in my heart

~~~

Sometimes I fancy the rapid flutter of tiny wings
Imagine the speckled bird returning
To settle on the mattress of moss
She shimmies down
Tucking in her oval darlings
Surely some day she will remember the secret portal
Canopied by bedstraw and spignel
Grown over with rockrose and forget-me-not

Summer after summer the chamber remains void

~~~

The vestigial moon slips beyond reach
Resurgent, she seeks the keening mountain
To rest her globe on its shoulder

Swiftly at my behest another dark fur-clad form
streaks across the hillside
Softly another muzzle comes to touch my knee
A new spirit, this
Not the longed-for re-visitation

~~~

Throughout the glen
Rings the echo
Of the cry of the lambs.

Clients and Therapists

About the Artists

Ross Symons - Cover Illustration

After having a real battle with my mental health, I found the outdoors became my new best friend. Walking in the woods, on the moors, and by the sea in my home city of Plymouth, gave me the release I needed and a real sense of purpose. I took up painting after it was recommended to me by an amazing counsellor, and I decided to combine the two.

The picture I created for the front cover of *Therapy in the Wild* shows that we all have a place within nature and the outdoors. It portrays all our wonderful local wildlife and birds waiting to welcome you, the reader, to take a seat and be serenaded by beautiful birdsong and entertained by cheeky squirrels.

I have been fortunate to have come through my dark times, and I continue to appreciate the living world around me.

Colin Michael Gersch - Interior Illustrations

Born in Horsham, Australia, in 1945, Colin Gersch was accepted as a student at the National Gallery of Victoria Art School in Melbourne in 1965, under the tutelage of John Brack.

After being awarded the 2nd year print prize, he was offered work as a scenic artist at Channel 9 to support his studies. Soon after, he moved into the design department full-time. In the following 33 years, Colin went on to design some of Australia's best-known light entertainment, comedy, music, drama, and awards programs for all the channels, in particular the ABC (Australian Broadcasting Corporation).

Colin says:

"My fascination and love of nature comes from my earliest childhood memories. Sitting by a spillway of an irrigation channel, legs dangling in the water, captivated by the willow tree roots that formed the bank; yabbies, dragonflies and later, the leeches firmly stuck to my legs, all initiated my empathy with the natural world."

About the Editor-in-Chief

Claire de la Varre, PhD, is a therapist, hypnotherapist, poet, and small group travel guide. This book is the first published under her own imprint, Positive Spiral Press.

www.positivespiralpress.com

Author Information

Here is contact information for the poets that have provided it:

Andrea Buckle
https://www.instagram.com/rhyndastonalpacas/
https://www.facebook.com/rhyndastonalpacas/

Brooke Conklin
youtube.com/@brookeconklin

Elaine Curtin
https://www.eleve-counselling.co.uk

Claire de la Varre, PhD
https://www.integrativehypnotherapy.uk
https://www.positivespiralhypnosis.com

Diana Thornton
https://www.surreyhillsmindfulness.co.uk
https://www.dianathornton.co.uk

Clients and Therapists